PREFACE

"I can immediately tell if someone is cut out for the world of PR. When someone first sits in my office, I will ask him or her to tell me what blogs they follow, what magazines they read and what is new in the world of PR. For example, I will see if they know every section of a magazine and see if they can dissect different media angles above and beyond just pitching the obvious. Public Relations in today's world is about looking at every part of the publication and seeing every single page that might feature your brand or your client. It takes a certain type of mind to see different angles and create a multitude of options that the naked eye would never notice. A true PR mindset is thinking publicity opportunities at all times. Unfortunately, PR it is not a function you can cut on and off, it just happens to be the way some of us look at the world."

~ Nicole K. Garner
(Founder / CEO)
The Garner Circle PR

ARE YOU [IN] INC.

PR's ALTER EGO
VOLUME 1.

FASHION PR | FILM PR | ENTERTAINMENT PR

BY NICOLE K. GARNER

PUBLISHED UNDER THE GARNER BRAND LLC.

ACKNOWLEGEMENTS

First and foremost I would like to thank my parents, Tommie and Rosalyn Garner, who did all they could do to foster my dreams – no matter how large, impractical and out of reach they may have sounded at the time of inception. A special thank you to all of my friends and family who executed patience with me as the world of PR carried me off to long hours behind the computer and made even the most patient of you, have to dig a little deeper and remain understanding with me. Thank you for always being such a strong support system thought the years. Thank you to my staff at The Garner Circle, who has worked diligently to make sure the agency, continues to grow and offer stellar PR/ publicity service especially my right hand executives Daniel Dickey and Eugenia Johnson. Thank you to all the incredible professionals who took time out from their busy schedule to provide their input, serving as such valuable resources. To my mentors who helped open doors, offered advice and different perspectives – I will forever be grateful. To my students who have taken my F.A.M.E. PR 101 workshops and attended my *PoweR Plug* PR Conferences (www.PowerPlugPR.com), who's hunger for knowledge served as the spark used to light the flame of this book coming to fruition. To our agency clients, it has been an honor making magic with you. To the members of the media, it has been such a pleasure working with you all. To the book designer and copy editor, thank you for seeing my vision.

XOXOXO - Nicole K. Garner

Are You **IN**? Inc.

Nicole Garner, founding principle of The Garner Circle PR and lifestyle marketing agency, has teamed up with fashion, film, entertainment and non- traditional PR and media elite to pen

Are You In, Inc.: *PR's Alter Ego* Book Series

vol.1 fashion | film | entertainment PR

A complete manual filled with everything you always wanted to know about the fabulous world of PR equipped with tools of the trade.
Order Today: **www.AreYouInInc.com/ebook**

This ultimate guide specializes in niche PR / publicity.

Includes [IN] terviews from:

BET.com
Janelle Monae
Wire Image
Sony Productions Unit Publicity
The Garner Circle PR
top bloggers & more...

" ...either you're IN or you're out!" ~ Heidi Klum

I have respect and deeply value a publicist who has strong morals, one, being a good and honest person. I also appreciate when a publicist understands your brand and won't bring forth any opportunities that are a disservice to your message and brand.

- Janelle Monae
Award winning recording artist

Why you should read
ARE YOU IN? INC.

"Rather than controlling the press, it is better to think in terms of managing It." ~ Nicole K. Garner

THE CONTENTS

TABLE OF CONTENTS

INTRODUCTION
- PART ONE: Minute 16 – Life beyond the first 15 Minutes of Fame   1
- PART TWO: The PR Toolkit   11
- PART THREE: Fashion PR   25
- PART FOUR: Film PR   41
- PART FIVE: Entertainment PR   61
- PART SIX: Digital, .Coms, PR 2.0 & Beyond...   71

Twitter: @TheGarnerCircle | Facebook.com/TheGarnerCirclePR | Youtube.com/TheGarnerCircle

INTRODUCTION

'It's never too late to start becoming what you were meant to be." ~George Eliot

So there you are preparing for graduation, or sitting behind your desk fantasizing about your ideal career. Would you gladly trade in your most prized possessions for your Vogue, Glamour, Vanity Fair and Elle magazine subscriptions? Are you a creative and innovative thinker? Is your cell phone constantly glued to your ear? Do you thrive on making connections, meeting new people, and developing ways to create buzz? You are a self-proclaimed social scientist, with a boatload of creative talent you just **CANNOT** let go to waste. If your finger is on the heart beat of everything that is hot, hip, and newsworthy, then you have decided to pick up this book for one of two reasons. The first being you are interested in delving into the world of publicity, the second you are looking for deeper understanding in the PR niche areas of fashion, film, and entertainment. This is the book I wanted when I was twenty- two years old and jumping into the world of publicity, wide – eyed and bushy tailed. After my PR course work in undergrad, I had the opportunity to take an amazing program at the Fashion Institute of Technology in New York, which specifically focused on fashion PR. That program fueled my

Thirst for more specific oriented knowledge on the "softer side" of PR. After many years of first- hand experiences, ground breaking campaigns, and my fair share of horror stories, looking back I realized that process did not have to be so long and tedious. I vowed that someday I would gather everything that I learned and share it with those who shared in this unexplainable adoration for this profession.

1

Minute 16

Life beyond the first fifteen minutes of fame...back to the basics

"Never stop evaluating your interests because they're bound to change over time, and that's okay. Better than okay, actually – it's human. I have never understood those people who, after fifteen years, are still sitting at the same desk, in the same cubicle, filing the same papers day after day. Be willing to challenge yourself to learn new things and, above all else, to take risks. I wouldn't be where I am right now if I'd gotten too comfortable with where I was before all this."

- Lindsey Skye Samuelsohn
(cofounder of Two Scoops via Shecky's)

What is the secret to fame and what makes an "it" product, person or brand? In the words of the beloved publicity igniter – Oprah Winfrey, "There is no such thing as luck, only being prepared when the opportunity presents itself". So in order to help you be prepared when the right media enticing opportunity presents itself, I have accumulated a list of PR / publicity basics to make sure you have a strong foundation to build upon.

XOXOXO
Nicole K. Garner

WHAT IS PR???

[IN layman's terms]

You see a gorgeous girl at a party.
You go up to her and say, "I am very rich. Marry me!"
That's Direct Marketing.

You're at a party with a bunch of friends and see a gorgeous girl.
One of your friends goes up to her and pointing at you says,
"He's very rich. Marry him."
That's Advertising.

You see a gorgeous girl at a party.
You go up to her and get her telephone number.
The next day you call and say, "Hi, I'm very rich. Marry me."
That's Telemarketing.

You're at a party and see a gorgeous girl.
You get up and straighten your tie; you walk up to her and pour her a drink. You open the door for her, pick up her bag after she drops it, offer her a ride, and then say,
"By the way, I'm very rich. Will you marry me?"
That's Public Relations.

You're at a party and see a gorgeous girl.
She walks up to you and says, "You are very rich."
That's Brand Recognition.

You're on your way to a party when you realize that there could be single women in all these houses you're passing. So you climb onto the roof of one situated toward the center and shout at the top of your lungs, "I'm rich. Marry Me!!!!
That's Spam.

You see a gorgeous girl at a party.
You go up to her and say, "I'm rich. Marry me"
She gives you a nice hard slap on your face.
That's Customer Feedback!

Publicity is the art of stirring up interest to promote your product or service
– Jay Levinson

"Public Relations helps an organization and its publics adapt mutually to each other."
- PRSSA

THE BREAKDOWN

Publicity operates both separate from and within the structure of almost any major corporation. Whether you work in fashion, film or entertainment, most large companies have an in-house publicity department as well as outside public relations, special events, or strategic marketing agency. Regardless of whether you work within a corporation or are hired on a contract basis, all publicists have a similar objective – to generate positive press, cut through the clutter, reach their target audience, and gain lasting popularity that transition into brand credibility and loyalty over time.

THE FLACKER ANATOMY

dose of energy

clipboard, smart phone, ipad, business cards

Account Executives (AE) – typically write press releases, create press kits, set up press photo shoots, develop PR campaigns and strategies. A day in the life of can consist of staying glued to the phone, pitching editors, producers, talk show talent bookers, and other gatekeepers and decision makers in the media industry.

Event Execustionist (EE) – typically handles movie premieres, fashion shows, store openings, product launches, cover parties, meet and greets, and more.

Procurement Specialists (PS) and producers – handle everything from the invitations, guest lists, celebrity attendance, venue scouting, sponsor tie – ins, red carpet management, photographers/ videographers, gift bags, and more.

The ultimate goal of a publicist is to...
Build a brand, generate great traditional and viral press, and satisfy the client.

SKILL SET
Skills you should definitely have when proceeding into niche specific PR:
- o Attention to detail
- o Creative and strategic thinking
- o Innovation
- o Excellent Follow Through
- o Writing Skills
- o Perfected networking skills
- o Pitching skills
- o Knowing the trade terminology, important dates, seasons, and a true understanding of the industry you are working in
- o Celebrity contacts (these come with time)
- o Attention to detail
- o People person
- o Thick skin
- o Ability to thrive under pressure
- o Organization skills
- o Ability to multitask
- o Be able to forecast and think ahead of the curve

THE PR TOOLKIT

Follow a Standard Press Release Format

Make sure your press release looks like a press release. The following can be used as a template for your press release.

Headline Is in Title Case and Short, Ideally Not More Than 170 Characters; This Headline Is 138 Characters Long and Does Not Take a Period

WHILE THE HEADLINE USES TITLE CASE, CAPITALIZING EVERY WORD EXCEPT FOR PREPOSITIONS AND ARTICLES OF THREE WORDS OR LESS, THE SUMMARY PARAGRAPH IS A LITTLE LONGER SYNOPSIS IN REGULAR SENTENCE FORM. IT DOESN'T MERELY REPEAT THE LEAD. IT JUST TELLS THE STORY IN A DIFFERENT WAY.

City, State (PRWEB) Month 1, 2005 -- The lead sentence contains the most important information in 25 words or less. Grab your reader's attention here. And don't assume that your reader has read your headline or summary paragraph; the lead should stand on its own.

A news release, like a news story, keeps sentences and paragraphs short, about three or four lines per paragraph. The first couple of paragraphs should cover the who, what, when, where, why and how questions.

The rest of the news release expounds on the information provided in the lead paragraph. It includes quotes from key staff, customers or subject matter experts. It contains more details about the news you have to tell, which can be about something unique or controversial or about a prominent person, place or thing.

"The final paragraph of a traditional news release contains the least newsworthy material," said Mario Bonilla, customer service representative for PR Web™. "But for an online release, it's typical to restate and summarize the key points with a paragraph like the next one."

For additional information on the news that is the subject of this release (or for a sample, copy or demo), contact Mary Smith or visit **www.prweb.com**. You can also include details on product availability, trademark acknowledgment, etc. here.

About XYZ Company:

Include a short corporate backgrounder about the company or the person who is newsworthy before you list the contact person's name and phone number. Do not include an e-mail address in the body of the release. Your e-mail address goes only in the "Contact e-mail" box when you first upload your press release.

Contact:

Mary Smith, director of public relations
XYZ Company
555-555-5555
http://www.YourWebAddress.com

Include safe harbour statement (if applicable).

###

© SOURCE PR WEB

TOOLS OF PUBLICITY

PRESS RELEASE

The press release tells the reader in-depth information about the product or person that you are representing. Preferably one page in length, the purpose of the press release is to get across the who, what, where, when, why and important details of the item that you are pitching. Next, the body must include all the important details the reader must know. Press releases should begin with a provocative, intriguing summary headline to give the essence of what is to follow. This headline should be in boldface and labeled "For Immediate Release". An interesting, relevant lead paragraph summarizes the story you are telling in the release. Always indicate if the release is two pages by using the word "more" at the bottom of the page and ### at the end of the release. In the world of fashion, a summary headline must be enticing enough so that it does not hit the infamous "waste basket". Remember to use the inverted triangle theory when constructing a news release, list facts in order of importance.

PRESS KIT

A cohesive branding and informational piece. Preferably in a physical, well graphically designed format or digital in a PDF format.

Components of a press kit:
- publicity photo
- packaging
- product overview
- fashion overview
- company history
- pitch letter
- press release
- bio
- fact sheets
- photography with caption
- press clippings
- testimonials
- options: celebrity endorsements save the date

Publicity Photos/ Line Sheets:
- should be submitted in high resolution format
- black and white are preferable
- attach credit and caption
- A line sheet is pages of sketches of the clothes showing sizes and pricing for buyers in a slick and professional format.

Press Conference:
A gathering held by a firm or an agency seeking publicity about an event or happening for news reporters.

Editorial Credit:

When publicity generated by fashion manufacturers appears in newspapers or magazines, it is the obligation of the editor to inform the readers where they can purchase the merchandise. The naming of retailers in such publicity is an editorial credit. The publicity may be featured within the fashion pages of the magazine, in an accompanying shopping guide at the rear of the publication, or listing where the merchandise is available.

Save – the- Date:
A one-page "short" sheet giving the reader succinct pre-information about a launch or event you are planning.

AFTER YOU HAVE DONE ALL YOU CAN DO, YOUR JOB IS NOT YET DONE…

After you distribute your press release, make your pitch calls, convince the media to take interest in your story - your job is not yet done. To successfully track your results and compile your results you will need to do the following:

Media Monitor - Collect press clippings; determine impressions, track online, viral, and social platform media hits. Record or note broadcast mentions and keep copies of advertisements and other branded materials. File this for your brand or present to the client, also present to event sponsors and key stakeholders as a record.

The PR Campaign

The Objective:
-To attract a new audience to your product
(i.e. boutique opening)

The Strategy:
-Increase college student shoppers by 50% within 6 months (must include quantitative goals)

The Tactics:
-Participating in college fashion shows
-Submitting press release to college media

CAMPAIGN PROCESS AND OUTLINE

I.   Statement of the Problem. In this section, you should explain the problem or opportunity that served (or will serve) as the focus of the campaign, including organizational history, issue history, current situation and problem statement. Assume that the reviewers of your paper know nothing about your chosen issue.

II. Research. In this section, you should discuss formative research used in planning the campaign.

III. Objectives. This section should identify and explain the campaign's intended purpose, including campaign goals and objectives. If designing a new campaign, your outcome objectives should be quantifiable, specifying the size and timeframe of the desired effect.

IV. Audiences, Messages and Media. This section should identify and describe primary and secondary target audiences, segmentation strategies, messages and media tactics.

V. Evaluation Strategies. This section should discuss summative research, or how you determined (or plan to determine) the extent to which campaign objectives are met.

TOOLS TO ENGAGE MEDIA:

- Editorial Meet and Greets
- Copy written for web-site content
- Introductions to fashion and accessory buyers
- Image Analysis
- Alliances with complimentary individuals or companies such as fashion stylists, boutiques, & other retail outlets
- Gift Bags, charity silent auctions and other promotional opportunities
- Celebrity Endorsement
- Editorial Placements digitally formatted
- Look Book Development
- Buzz Worthy Press Kits

PR WIRE SERVICES:
PR web | Pitchengine

PHOTO WIRE SERVICES:
Wire image | Getty images

MEDIA DATABASES
Vocus | Cision | Burelles

Special Events

These events can be used to generate publicity and draw in media interest:

- o Product Launch / Film Junket

- o Grand Openings

- o Soft Grand Opening

- o Trunk Show / Media Preview

- o Trade Show

- o Twitter | Faceboook Media Engagement

3

FASHION PR

"Fashion is not something that exists in dresses only. Fashion is in the sky, in the street, fashion has to do with ideas, the way we live, what is happening." ~ Coco Chanel

WHAT DO FASHION EDITORS WANT FROM YOU?

The key to any successful PR campaign starts with understanding your audience. Before your product or service ever makes it to the pages of a popular magazine or newspaper, it must first pass a strenuous test conducted solely by a beauty editor. If you cannot catch their attention then you will never make it to the consumer. In order to attract the editor's attention it is important that you know a little about the person you're dealing with.

Once you have a good understanding of whom you will be pitching to, you must study each publication to find out who their audience is and what stories would work best for their format. Knowing a little about the publication will also help you to custom tailor your pitches for each individual outlet. For example, if you're trying to promote a new miracle cream for stretch marks, you should change your script when pitching to a fitness magazine versus a pregnancy publication. To get a better understanding of the different magazines start by studying the publishing houses.

There are five main publishers including Conde Nast, Hachette Filipacchi Media, Hearst, Fairchild and Time Inc. Under Conde Nast you have publications such as Vogue, Allure, Glamour, GQ, Lucky and Vanity Fair.

Each publication looks for different types of stories, but they all follow the same criteria for pitching. First, you should know that editors generally work on a three-month lead-time. That means if you are pitching a product in September the editor is usually working on their January issue, therefore your product should be geared toward that season. If you only have one product and it doesn't really fit in with the season that an editor is working on, it is up to you to put a spin on it so that it does fit. Editors also only want things that are NEW.

If a product has been seen in other magazines then the editor will probably choose not to cover it again. It's best to pitch one product or rime at the same time to all of the publications. For example, on the first week we might choose to pitch our new mud facial and then go from there by introducing additional products or services. Keep in mind that if you are pitching a product, editors like full-size products. Never give them small samples or images, unless requested. Otherwise, your product may find its way in the back of the editorial closet or at the bottom of the trashcan.

The Process
The first step to getting a placement in any magazine is to pitch the editor a product or service. You can do this a number of different ways including sending information/products via messenger, having a desk side meeting where you meet with the editor face to face or you can send materials the old fashioned way- snail mail.

Missing the Story

You can send products and pitch stories to editors until you're blue in the face, but at the end of the day you still may not get your story. This is to be expected, especially in the first few months, but if it continues there are a few things you should take into consideration. First, you must have a story to tell. If you don't have anything new to tell the editors then they are going to cover the company that does.

How They Like It

Now that you know what to expect from a beauty editor and what is involved in the basic process of having your product or service placed, it is important to know what it takes to complete a story. When sending anything to an editor you should always include a press kit. Press kits come in a variety of styles, but a good kit always includes some basics. First, the price of each product or service being pitched should be listed in a press release or price sheet. Next, you should include locations for purchase, a toll free number and website. It also helps to include a celebrity list, if available, and a fact sheet on who, what, where, when and why. Lastly, visuals always help make the sale. This may include product shots or photos of people receiving a service.

Something New, Nothing Old

Editors always want to be the first to cover the latest trends. They are looking for unheard of ingredients to a story line. Especially in the day and age of social media & digital publications/blogs, every minute counts and story angles lose timeliness at an exponential rate.

Creating a Story

One thing that separates the products that get placed from those that don't is the extra step a company takes to build a story. Successful companies do whatever they can to make an editor's job easier.

Star Buzz

It's already been said that celebrities can help push a story to fruition, but keep in mind that you shouldn't state that a celebrity is using your product or service unless you can prove it. Most legitimate publications will ask for a letter on your company letterhead stating that the celebrity does use the product or service. They may even ask for a proof of purchase. And don't be surprised if the editor fact checks with the celebrity's publicist.

The Art of Following Up

If you have gone through the trouble to follow all the steps mentioned above you must do one more thing. Follow up. It is essential that you speak with the editor once you've sent a product. We have a saying in our agency – the "P" in PR stands for persistence.

Remember that all editors are hired to report what is true, available and newsworthy. If you work with them, educate them and keep them up-to-date with your beauty accomplishments, you are sure to make it into their publication. Building these relationships take time, but following the simple guidelines laid out here will help ensure your success.

THE **IN**TERVIEW LOUNGE

Kimberly Walker
Beauty & fashion Editor
Has worked for BET.com, Ebony.com, 944 Magazine & More

HER PERSPECTIVE

I've come to learn a few things about beauty and style editors. **1.** We're totally obsessed with our industries. **2.** We love finding others who are equally obsessed. What does this mean in relation to you as a publicist? Be a part of your product's movement. Things like lip gloss and scarves truly excite us, so when you perform your pitch - in person or via email - know that we're looking for the "wow" factor. What makes your product different? Can you give me significant details versus just simply suggesting that I do a write up because it is mascara and I write beauty?

Media Ins & Outs - You should know the media just as well as you know your clientele. Understanding the demographic and voice of your selected media outlet will not only help you attain a well-respected "co-sign" for your client, but also concretely tap into your fan base. When publicists pitch me things to potentially cover in the areas of beauty and style, I look to see if they understand two things: our readers and our price point. For instance, if you do your research on the demographics of BET.com/Lifestyle, you'll find that our site resonates more with the young, trendy population of a multi-cultural American landscape, specifically 18 - 24 and largely female. It would not be wise to pitch a new anti-aging cream, because regardless of how wonderful it may be, African-American females age 18 - 24 are not concerned about wrinkles. However, they are obsessed with having perfect skin, so a cream that promises to clear acne and fade scars would be optimal. Also, do your research on the average product price and potential salaries of that publication's readers. If the highest priced pair of shoes evens out around $300, your fabulous new client's $900 pair of pumps might not be a fit.

The Almighty Freebie... - Of course editors like receiving free stuff. Who does not? But it is not just about making your friends jealous about all the sweet treats you receive in the mail. Understand that giving the writer a visual, scent, or touch, enhances their ability to write more about your product. For example, a look book for a designer's spring collection is great to view and develop ideas, however there's nothing like watching the ensemble strut down the catwalk. Always demo your product. If you represented a budding singer, you would not simply send a few facts about your rising star, you would provide a taste for the ears to sample.

The Prettier the Package... - Presentation is everything. In the past, I have run stories on designers and beauty lines simply because I was in complete awe of their creative packaging (and it was a fit for the publication, of course). Show editors that you are willing to invest time and money into their valued opinion. After interviewing Lisa Price, founder of Carol's Daughter, she sent me a gift because I briefly mentioned that I got a whiff of her delicious Pearl perfume and later received a compliment due to my in-store squirt. Both Price and her publicist are so accommodating and nice, I find myself plugging her line every chance I get.

Do's and Don'ts... - DO pitch products according to the seasons. If it is a print publication, pitch potential spring/summer stories by January or February. Online properties have a variety of timelines, but generally keep their calendars fairly open to accommodate the rapidly changing trends in beauty and style news. Simply check with an editor. DON'T pitch a premature product or line to a nationally ran publication, or any publication, for that matter. Take the time to ensure that your aesthetics read "professional" and "prepared." You run the risk of being discarded in the future due to your ill-timed proposal.

Lastly, have fun and really believe in your clients. It always makes the difference.

- THE END -

THE FASHION SHOW

FRONT OF THE HOUSE PR

➢ Oversee the mailing and delivery of invitations by coordinating with a mail house, post office and messenger service.

➢ RSVPs / Seating Charts

➢ Install and monitor individual designer RSVP hotline and computerized designer invitation database.

➢ Seating of fashion shows: pre-seating, soliciting RSVPs and providing seating assignments.

➢ Coordinate all necessary front of house staff including check-in, seating and security

➢ Hire runway photographer, digital photographer, video crew and/or backstage photographer.

➢ Meet and greet press, retail, celebrities and socialites.

➢ PR Firms may also assist in: market research; audience identification; visual merchandising; direct marketing; sponsorship; press releases; electronic media; publicity and advertising; and the primary purpose---merchandising the product

BACK OF THE HOUSE PR

➤ Oversee the backstage production, including referral of professional dressers, arrange clothing transportation, coordinate catering, music, lighting, etc.

➤ Coordinate all staff including hair, stylist, make up, dressers, models and vendors.

➤ Stage design and production

FASHION SHOW PLANNING & LOGISTICS

Initial Planning
- Who is your target market?
- Determine your budget; get quotes
- Find a venue
- Find out if you need lighting, sound, cleanup crew, insurance, audio/visual person, security, etc.
- Obtain sponsors
- Set a date

FASHION SHOW SEATING PROTOCOL

FRONT ROW – Editors and Chief of Major Magazines, fashion and creative directors, major buyers, celebrities and media influencers (i.e.global bloggers, socialites)

SECOND ROW – fashion directors/ senior fashion editors from national newspapers, bloggers & online media with massive traction

THIRD ROW – Regional media and fashion director assistants

FOURTH ROW – local media, boutique buyers, sponsors

FIFTH ROW – Important people to the designer

STANDING ROOM - Fashion Students, etc.

Fashion PR Specifics

THE FASHION CLOSET

Remember the scene on Sex and the City I – the movie, where Carrie Bradshaw started her new job in the offices of Vogue and walked into the fashion closet. This is where ready-to-photograph product resides sent in by PR agents in efforts to be included in a feature or spread.

YOUR "[IN]dustry" FRIENDS:

✓ Editors and writers, can make mention of fashionable pieces or tie your client into trend stories

✓ Stylist – can place your clients product on celebrities or get them featured spreads

46

Film PR

"lights...camera...action...ink!"

Press and publicity play a vital role in the marketing of films. Press campaigns are carefully planned in advance and encompass both Unit Publicity (carried out during the film shoot) and Distribution Publicity (arranged to coincide with the film's release).

These two areas require different specialist skills and usually involve two different experts or Publicity companies.

Unit Publicists are hired by Producers, Distributors or Sales Agents and together they plan appropriate press strategies involving regional, national and international media, including Newspapers, Magazines, Radio, Terrestrial and Satellite Television, Internet Broadcasting, etc. During filming, Unit Publicists work closely with 1st and 2nd Assistant Directors to ensure that actors and selected crew members are available for interviews, and help journalists and EPK (Electronic Press Kit) crews to schedule and conduct interviews.

Unit Stills Photographers work closely with the Unit Publicist to ensure that sufficient good quality photographic stills are taken during the shoot. This is an important part of the Publicity process, and can make the difference between a newspaper or magazine editor deciding whether or not to run a piece. EPK crews are hired by Studios, Distributors, Sales Agents, or sometimes Unit Publicists, to produce interviews and behind the scenes footage of feature films. These segments are edited and transferred onto Broadcast Video Tape, CD, DVD or VHS formats, and supplied to broadcasters as a package.

Although the various Publicity roles require specific areas of expertise, all those working in Unit Publicity must be capable of pitching and selling ideas, and need a good understanding of what journalists and editors require from stories, excellent communication skills, the ability to work well under pressure, and good organizational skills.

Unit Publicists (UPs) provide a vital conduit between Producers, cast, crew and the media during film shoots. By generating publicity, they help Sales Agents to sell films and to create public interest. UPs work closely with Producers, Distributors and Sales Agents to plan all press strategy for film shoots, making sure that only the right amount of information is released at specific times, so that the press coverage is not jeopardies when the film is released.

UPs are responsible for Unit press and publicity budgets that are set by Producers. UPs work on a freelance basis, and are hired only for the duration of each shoot, although they may also be employed to handle distribution publicity in the run-up to the film's release date.

What is the job?

Unit Publicists (UPs) start work on films between 4 to 6 weeks before the first day of principal photography. Their first responsibility is to issue a press release providing information about the film to selected press, and to ensure that details about the film shoot; cast and crew are printed in the Trade Press. Once the shooting schedule has been agreed, UPs work with the Producer, and often with the Actors' Agents (or Managers) to schedule visits to the set, on specific shooting days, by a number of selected journalists, who may represent a mixture of magazines, and regional, national and international newspapers and broadcasters.

UPs ensure that the Actors and Director are available to the journalists on these days, and that there is plenty happening to provide a good color piece (an article that sets the scene and is full of lively descriptions of the set, etc.) The UP and the journalists, or sometimes the newspaper/magazine editors, discuss when each article will be published in order to maximize the film's publicity. During a set visit, UPs liaise with the 2nd Assistant Director to check actors' schedules and to deal with any last minute changes, which often occur on film sets, and help to facilitate the journalists' work. UPs may also work closely with the EPK (Electronic Publishing Kit) Crew.

UPs are also responsible for: the production of films' press packs, which involves interviewing cast and crew members (UPs may undertake these interviews themselves or hire a journalist to do so); preparing a comprehensive list of cast and crew; writing a long and a short synopsis of the film; writing production notes (containing information about the work histories of the Writer, Director, Production Designer, Costume Designer, Script Writer and key cast members).

UPs usually oversee the work of the Unit Stills Photographer with whom they work closely, selecting the best days for the photographer to be on set. After the film has wrapped (been completed), UPs must provide captions for all the photographs, and ensure that the agreed number of color and black and white prints/negatives are delivered to the production or Distributor.

Typical Career Routes

Although there is no typical career route for this role, good UPs must have excellent contacts within the film media, and it is vital to begin building these links as early in their careers as possible. UPs may gain experience working for Film Press and Public Relations Companies, starting as junior Assistants and progressing to more senior roles. Alternatively, they may work their way up from Assistant levels in the Publicity department of Film/Distribution Companies.

Experience can also be gained by working in the Press offices of Arts organizations, broadcasters and film festivals. In-house Press Offices (of Film Production or Distribution Companies) and Film PR Companies advertise Office Junior or Assistant roles in the media pages of national newspapers, and in the jobs pages of the Trade Press.

Essential Knowledge and Skills

UPs must be computer literate and have excellent knowledge of all film media (regional, national and international) and of the tastes and opinions of specific film journalists. They should have an understanding of the demographics of publications (and broadcasters) and be able to tie this in to their knowledge of film markets. They must also have excellent contacts and good working relationships with key personnel in the film and media industries.

Key Skills include:

- Ability to pitch and sell ideas
- Understanding of what journalists and editors need from a story
- Understanding of Producers'/Directors' ambitions for films
- Excellent literacy skills
- Effective communication skills
- Diplomacy and tact
- Ability to work well under pressure
- Good organizational skills
- Knowledge of the requirements of the relevant Health and Safety legislation and procedures

Training and Qualifications

Although there is no specific training for this job, UPs are usually graduates of English, Arts, Theatre, Communications, Media or Film Studies courses. Individual course accreditation in certain subject areas is currently being piloted. As part of Skillset's and the UK Film Council's Film Skills Strategy, A Bigger Future, a network of Screen Academies and a Film Business Academy have been approved as centers of excellence in education and training for film. For more information, please log onto the Skillset website.

Publications

Regional, national and international newspapers, magazines, radio, the internet and broadcast media all feature reviews by regular critics. Screen International is a weekly publication for the film industry, which also offers a daily on-line news service. Screen Daily Variety is a weekly publication for the film, television, music and interactive entertainment industries. Variety Campaign is a magazine containing news and articles about the media industry. Sight and Sound is another monthly magazine featuring articles, reviews and full credit lists for international cinema.

EPK Director / Producer

EPKs (Electronic Press Kits) are press kits produced in Broadcast Video Tape, CD, DVD or VHS formats and are vital components of the unit publicity generated during film shoots. The most basic EPKs consist of a collection of interviews with key cast and crew members, and some behind the scenes footage, plus in some cases a selection of final film clips, and possibly the theatrical trailer.

EPK Producers are also responsible for other publicity materials such as "making-of" documentaries for the domestic and international market, "extras" for the DVD release, and promotional material for the film's website. There are usually three practitioners on EPK Crews: Director/Producer, Camera Operator and Sound Mixer.

However, as the quality of smaller DV cameras improves they can be used as a less intrusive and more economical means of shooting the behind the scenes shots (b rolls), thereby reducing the crew to one or two practitioners. EPKs are produced and edited by a small number of highly specialist companies who employ Director/Producers (D/Ps) to write and edit each production. Camera and Sound Operators are hired on a film-by-film basis, and are usually highly experienced film industry practitioners. EPK D/Ps often work on three or four films simultaneously.

The Tools

THE PRESS JUNKET
A post-screening one-on-one publicity interview marathon between the media and a production's director and lead actors.

THE WORLD OF FILM PUBLICITY INCLUDES

- Writing and Distribution of Press Releases

- Pitching Media Specifically Targeted to the Audience You Want to Reach

- Coordinating Interviews

- Film Festival Press Coverage

- Placement of "Experts" in Various Media Outlets

- Set / Unit Publicity

- New Product Launches

- Press Kit Preparation, Including the Selection of Photos

- Film Clip Selection

- Coordinating Press Screenings

- Coordinating Media Tours

- Escorting and Introduction to Press and Red Carpet Events

- Handling the movie critic – traditional media, the blogger, and social media influencers

THE **IN**TERVIEW LOUNGE

Arian Simone

Project Publicist for Sony & Rainforest Films |
Creator of Fearless Magazine

HER PERSPECTIVE | *My Journey To Movie PR*

I moved to Los Angeles with a job, after one month of employment, the company get sold; I was laid off and had no money. I moved from my apartment I could no longer afford my car. I sold my clothes and belongings so I could eat and put gas in my car. Never would I have imagined that all this would happen to me! I was full of education, undergraduate school, graduate school and no job. I applied for over 150 plus jobs and no one hired me. I tried temp agencies, I was on welfare, food stamps; car broke down, checked into a shelter, etc. Through the trial my relationship with Christ grew very strong. I was with out a place to live for 7 months. Fortunately, someone who knew of me from my previous job that year referred me to his or her spouse for some PR & Marketing work. I immediately got the car out of the shop, and then moved into an office space with the help of my sorority sister ND Brown.

Then one day Coach Carter (the real Coach Carter the movie Coach Carter was based off) was on my floor and he introduced me to the fact that movie studios outsource people for what I do. He had me help out with some things for the movie prior to its release. From this exposure I then contacted people who were FAMU alumnus (Will Packer and Rob Hardy) that I knew were in the movie business and informed them about what I had been up to and I was blessed with an interview opportunity with Sony Pictures and was able to work on STOMP THE YARD!

MY SPECIALTY

Though I have worked on a variety of projects, I specialize in Urban Market Publicity and Promotions. How someone is perceived in the Urban Market and how someone is perceived in the Mainstream Market can be the same and in some cases it may differ. When seeking coverage in order to promote a film, this is very important to understand someone's current position in the market. I take time to evaluate cast members current positioning in order to seek maximum exposure.

FUNNY STORY

One time when I was conducting an EPK interview on a movie set we had to stop the interview because there were airplanes flying above us so it caused noise interference. The talent got upset and wanted me to stop the planes, he said you have a reputation of getting things, you can't stop the planes? I apologized, but the wild part about it, he really thought I could stop the planes. Maybe he expected me to call air traffic control, I don't know but thank God we eventually got the interview done.

SUCCESS STORY

After success with the STOMP THE YARD campaign my company was blessed to work THIS CHRISTMAS, QUANTUM OF SOLACE 007, HANCOCK, SEVEN POUNDS, FIRST SUNDAY, TAKING OF PELHAM 1 2 3, and the list goes on! We have serviced plenty of celebrities from Lil Wayne to Chris Brown and have put on some very star studded and grand events surrounding the Oscars and Grammys. I give God the Glory, Honor and Praise for all my accomplishments, as it has been His hand doing all the work!

ARIAN'S DAY IN THE LIFE OF A FILM PUBLICIST & USEFUL NUGGETS:

Hire your still photographer

Hire your EPK crew

Document your case studies

Read the script - if its action or drama (draw from the script what values and topics that stand out (love, rivalry, family) go by the shooting schedule and see which days you want the EPK crew on set
(all the work that will be publicized later)

Determine days dedicated to being press days (print, online, TV camera crew). Never schedule top tier outlets on the same day, give them their own day to come on set. (make sure you schedule on a day when everyone is there), look at call sheets to make sure everyone is there on that day, and what times actors arrive to set on that day

- Always alert cast that the press is coming on set

- Send your name and contact to the production secretary and demand that
  they send all press inquires to you

- It is key that press does not leak unauthorized footage it can kill a
  project

- Officially introduce yourself to the staff

- Provide all actors with memos of their talking points (with larger actors run these
  past their publicist)

- Keep a very strict paper trail

- Massage egos of the actor's publicist and make sure they are well informed

- Stay in tuned with the production

- Release campaign media junkets

- Give the still photographer a list of mandatory shots

- The producers knows how they want the movie to be betrayed - the show and which celebs are promoted creates the feel of the movie

5

Entertainment PR

"When posing for paparazzi always stand on the right." ~ SocialDiva.com

"Because entertainment never sleeps, Entertainment Publicists simultaneously live 24 / 7 career lifestyles." – Nicole Garner

Connecting the Dots….

Being in the know, getting clients on red carpets, interview exposure, parties that will attract more media attention, capitalizing on buzz…. this is just the beginning of entertainment publicity.

Preparing your client for the interview….

Media Training

THE DO'S

- Be yourself. An interview is not the time to change your style or become theatrical.

- Take a deep breath before you begin speaking to fill your lungs with air and help get rid of that nervous edge in your voice.

- Listen carefully to the questions being asked, use simple language.

- Speak slowly and clearly, especially for radio or television interviews.

- Repeat your key points. At the end of the interview, summarize your main points for the reporter.

- Prepare a fact sheet & talking points in advance with relevant information and statistics. Give a copy to the reporter to ensure you are not misunderstood or misquoted.

- If asked several questions at once, pick the one question you want to answer and let the reporter re-ask the others.
- Prepare for the interview by asking for topics to be covered. Practice your answers to anticipated questions.

- Comment only on matters in which you have expertise and authority.

THE DON'TS

- Be very careful about going "off the record" or trying to make deals about what may or may not be reported. The only way to guarantee something is never repeated is never to say it in the first place.

- If a question contains negative language, don't repeat it in your answer.

- Don't assume the reporter is an expert in your industry. Avoid jargon.

- Don't look at the camera. Maintain steady eye contact with the reporter.

- Don't limit yourself to questions being asked. To get your key points presented, you may have to rephrase a question.

- Never speculate about an answer.

- Don't allow a reporter to put words in your mouth.

- Never interrupt the reporter. Your goal should be to establish a good rapport.

- Don't expect to be permitted to review or edit a story before it goes to press.

- Inform, don't sell. While it may represent an opportunity to get publicity for your business, an interview is not an ad or a sales call.

Red Carpet Etiquette

Working a client on the red carpet:

Understand red carpet timing (A list celebrities will take precedence)

Sticking to your time schedule (usually the awards PR team has taken into consideration perfect timing for your client)

Mapping out and identifying outlets

Monitoring Interviews and keeping them swift

Managing the red carpet

Position top tier outlets

Placing long interview outlets towards the end as to not hold up red carpet traffic

Allow photos and stills first, then proceed with interviews

Control chaos at all times

Bringing in the fire works !!!

Hire a Wire Service photographer to source photos

Incorporate a Step and Repeat – a photo opportunity banner that contains the event branding and sponsorship logos. Photos sourced will provide visibility for sponsors and encourage visibility for the event.

ALWAYS create a mandatory shot list for photographer & b-roll video crew

Entertainment Publicist Society

1. A member shall respect and support the highest standards of accuracy and truth in all business activities.

2. A member shall give credit for ideas and words borrowed from others and only accept credit for work personally performed.

3. A member shall never knowingly communicate false or misleading information and will act promptly to correct any misinformation discovered.

4. A member shall not intentionally damage the professional reputation or practice of another practitioner, member or not.

5. A member shall safeguard the confidences and privacy rights of all present and former clients and employers.

6. A member shall not provide a media representative with anything that could be construed as an inducement toward favorable or preferential treatment.

7. A member shall not guarantee the achievement of specified objectives resulting from any program or campaign implemented by the member.

8. A member shall not represent conflicting or competing clients without the express consent of those concerned.

SOURCE: http://www.bollingerpr.com/EPPS.htm#COE

6

Digital, .Coms, P R 2.0 & Beyond…

Pitching Online Media

In today's PR landscape, online media helps provide immediate coverage and results. Online media has a greater need for content with more daily and multi-daily options.

Taking the traditional press release and making it applicable to social media platforms.

Social Media newswires such as pitchengine.com assist with the following not only distributing the press release to traditional outlets but reaching media in a multitude of communication channels and assists with Search Engine Optimizations (SEO).

TIPS:

+ Get a front row seat at the viral "Conversation". Conversation will take place surrounding a brand whether the PR team gets engaged or not. It is better to be proactive and be on the front end of the "viral talk". Get engaged with Twitter/ Facebook/ Youtube.com/ Linked In/ Pinterest/ Instragram as a part of your PR duties.

+ Do not abuse social media
  - Do not use social media as a means of "spamming" the media

+ Track ROI & Impressions through social media campaigns and strategy (tracking engines include Monitter and Statigram)

+ With platforms such as TWITTER, incorporate the use of the Hashtag (#_____) and utilize twitter search to track traction

+ Increase audiences and engagement by streaming video

+ Owned Media
  - Now publicists do not have to wait for the middleman. Service content and messaging though owned websites, social media platforms, blogs and more

+ Blogger Pet Peeves
  "When publicist send long recaps" - Sandrarose.com

Online Reputation Management (ORM) in Social Media:

The "Age of Engage" is now—and today you must join the conversation via top social media networks and micro-blogging services if you want to drive real results for your brand. That's because tools like Twitter, Facebook, LinkedIn and other emerging social networks give you the ability to reach your customers and stakeholders directly. The numbers are staggering: Facebook reaches over 400 million users—with more than three million active brand and fan pages, more than 1.5 million local businesses with pages on Facebook, and 20 million people becoming fans of pages daily for a total of 5.3 billion fans. LinkedIn claims 60 million users—and leaked reports suggest that Twitter projects 1 billion users by 2013.

Put simply: The possibilities for marketers and communicators are limitless. However, as we're seeing with Nestle, social media comes with great responsibility. So how can you best incorporate these channels into into programs to get the word out about your companies or products? How do you protect your brand reputation in a democratized online society? What are the nation's top companies doing right to drive engagement, buzz and brand online—and what best practices can you learn from them?

(Source PR University)

Social Media is a very opinionated world – as a publicist you can't control it, your client's will have to learn to let go and organically connect
-   James Andrews [CNN social media expert]

THE **IN**TERVIEW LOUNGE

Tiffany Davis

Has worked for DailyCandy.com & NBC

HER PERSPECTIVE   *DEALING WITH THE MEDIA*

Tiffany Davis is a stylist, writer, and editor based currently based in New York City, was hired to launch DailyCandy.com's Atlanta edition in March of 2006. She has written, reviewed, and blogged for publications including Glamour, Allure, and Brides.com. She has appeared as a culture and style expert on CNN, TBS, CBS, AOL and Fox5 Atlanta and now works at NBC.

WHAT PR TACTICS IMRESS YOU: As a member of the media, we are very impressed when you can tell us something we don't know. We are not impressed when you tell us something everyone already knows. We are positively insulted when you tell us about something that we ourselves said/featured/discussed/critiqued and try to pass it off as an original concept. Read us. Stalk us. Google us. Craft pitches with us in mind as well as your client.

If you aspire to create something new, do your research. If you're going to knock something off, do it better than what's already out there. Don't send endless samples. Don't use bribes as a pitching tactic. Don't ever, ever promise exclusives that you can't deliver. We hate being mass-emailed. Chances are we did read that e-mail (and the follow-up) but maybe we just didn't love it for what we were working on at the time. If good images and a short press release can't sell us on a story, all of the follow-up in the world won't change our minds.

Whether you're a freelancer, publicist, designer, or aspiring to be any one of those things, keep the following in mind: Editors want to like the story that you're selling them. We wake up in the morning hoping that we'll discover dozens of stories, fruitful leads, and awesome new sources. Help us help you.

ABOUT THE AUTHOR
[NICOLE K. GARNER]

"I can count on Nicole & The Garner Circle PR to listen to my needs as an artist and pull together as many different fitting opportunities/brands as possible to help further my mission and message. What I love about The Garner Circle is they cater to your needs and customize their services for you. When it is time to plan an event and get the word out or partner with a charity, etc., I know that The Garner Circle PR will see to it that all details are taken care of and that everyone is happy, each step of the way. Honestly, I never have to worry when working with The Garner Circle PR."
~ Janelle Monae (Award Winning Songstress and Cover Girl Spokesperson)

A young PR flacker best described as...

a pretty powerful publicist. **idea architec**t. flacker. **decisive maven**. style enthusiast. serial entrepreneur. visionaire. **influencer.** healthy lifestylist. vintage modernist. trend forecaster. action dreamer. **big picture thinker.** author. speaker. art appreciator. global adventurist. woman of Alpha Kappa Alpha Sorority Inc. activist. cool hunter. **female empowerer.**

Nicole Garner is the founder & CEO of The Garner Circle PR & The Garner Brand LLC having worked with celebrities to include Keri Hilson, Janelle Monae, Moet, and brands to include MillerCoors, Strength of Nature and more.

She is a product of Georgia State University and the Fashion Institute of Technology.

THE ARE YOU [IN] INC
BOOK SERIES

Vol. 1 fashion | film | entertainment
Vol. 2 beauty | sports | non- profit
& more to come ....

Media Contact:
The Garner Circle PR
E: PR@TheGarnerCircle.com

[COMING SOON!]

10 THINGS YOUR MOM NEVER TOLD YOU ABOUT BEING A FEMALE ENTREPRENEUR©

a power girl's guide

pretty POWERFUL

INSIGHT BY FELICIA JOY
ms.ceo.
Be savvy. Be profitable. Be bold!

by nicole garner
THEGARNERBRAND | THEGARNERCIRCLEPR
ILLUSTRATION BY AARON THE ARTIST

Don't just chase your dreams... stalk them!

Before taking the dive as fierce female into the pool of entrepreneurism, I developed this comic-style guide to serve as a "Cliff's Notes" approach to practical advice that will help any young woman on her journey to following her dreams and creating her own future."10 Things Your Mom Never Told You About Being a Female Entrepreneur" gives tips for the emerging power girl as she flourishes in the world of business and womanhood as a whole. I gathered these tips from first-hand experience and personal trial & error. As a female, there are things that only we as women experience in the world of entrepreneurism. I want this guide to serve as a starting point for you, making sure you are better prepared not only in regards to business savy but emotionally as well. Always remember, the best way to predict the future is to create it. For more information on where the guide is available visit www.TheGarnerBrand.com/PrettyPowerful .

Love & Kisses,
Nicole Garner
[The Garner Circle PR | The Garner Brand]
f: prettypowerful t: #PrettyPowerful @TheGarnerCircle

ARE YOU **IN**? Inc.

"PR's alter ego" by nicole k. garner

"...either you're IN or you're out" ~ Heidi Klum

www.TheGarnerCircle.com | twitter.com/thegarnercircle

GET SOCIAL:
T/IG: @TheGarnerCircle / @tgcPRagency #AreYouInInc
RESOURCES: PoweR Plug PR Conference www.PowerPlugPR.com

23140251R00047

Made in the USA
Charleston, SC
14 October 2013